Distant Valleys

Poems of Chŏng Chi-Yong

Translated
by
Daniel A. Kister

기   증

이   번역작품집은   한국문화예술진흥원의
문예진흥기금   지원으로   출판되었습니다.
[한국문학의   세계화]를   위하여
널리   활용하여   주시면   고맙겠습니다.

ASIAN HUMANITIES PRESS
Berkeley, California

ASIAN HUMANITIES PRESS

Asian Humanities Press offers to the specialist and the general reader alike, the best in new translations of major works and significant original contributions, to enhance our understanding of Asian literature, religions, cultures and thought.

Cover Photo: Landscape by Shim Sa Chŏng (1707-1769)
Courtesy Sogang University Museum

Library of Congress Cataloging-in-Publication Data

Chŏng, Chi-yong, b. 1903.
 Distant valleys: poems of Chŏng Chi-yong / translated by
Daniel A. Kister.
  p.   cm.
 "The present translations are based on the revised edition of
'The collected works of Chŏng Chi-yong, I: Poetry (Seoul:
Minŭmsa, July 1988)"—Pref.
 Includes indexes.
 ISBN 0-87573-032-9
 1. Chŏng, Chi-yong, b. 1903—Translations. I. Kister,
Daniel A. II. Title.
PL991.2.C4A24 1994
895.7'14—dc20   93-51018
                                                       CIP

Contents

For Ann and Nancy

Introduction

The cornucopia of poetry that enriched the world's store of literature between World War I and World War II includes not only works by such well-known English and European authors as Yeats, Eliot, Frost, Pound, Rilke, and Valéry, but also works by Korean poets that most western readers have never heard of. One of these, Chŏng Chi-yong, published between 1926 and 1950 a small but remarkable body of verse that deserves to rank with the best poetry of the period in richness of feeling and ripeness of imagination.

Chŏng Chi-yong's poems breathe the air of the village, sea, and mountains of the Korean peninsula. They express attitudes which Koreans have long treasured as their own: a loving closeness to nature and other human beings; an appreciation of truths implicit in the heart's endless longing; a fondness for playful humor and childlike wonder; a tendency toward indirectness and ambiguity; and a predilection for drawing beauty out of the commonplace. Typically Korean but not at all exotic, Chŏng's countryside has a more authentic rural feel than the masked pastoralism of the American poet Robert Frost; but like Frost, Chŏng draws the reader into a particular locale whose horizons are universal. Not exclusively Korean or rural, the affection, longing, humor, and wonder that characterize Chŏng's work are rooted in commonplaces of the human heart.

Chŏng's closest poetic kin in the West are perhaps Ezra Pound and William Butler Yeats. Chŏng does not load his poetry with allusions like Pound or with the conceptual questioning that Yeats is prone to. But as his work matures, he achieves, like Pound, a mastery of crisp, suggestive images; and like Yeats, he fashions varied patterns of imagery and sound that brim with human affection and love of life. He

1

could well say, like Yeats in "The Circus Animals' Desertion," that all his poetry begins in the "rag and bone shop of the heart."

Chŏng Chi-yong was born in Ch'ungchŏng Province in 1902, the oldest son of a dealer in Chinese medicine. Chi-yong was raised in the Catholic faith and according to the custom of the time was married when he was only twelve years old. He knew poverty as a child, but through the graces of a benefactor was able to attend Hwimun Secondary School in Seoul. With his school comrades, he there began his poetic activities. He also took part in a protest movement within the school, for which he was temporarily suspended. Upon graduation in 1922, he went to Japan to do university studies in English Literature, writing a thesis on William Blake.

Chŏng may have published a couple of poems in 1922 or 1923, but he began publishing in earnest in 1926 at the age of twenty-five. Upon returning to Korea after graduation in 1929, he began teaching English at his high-school alma mater. He continued in this position until the end of the Japanese occupation and World War II in 1945, all the while continuing to publish poetry. During various periods between 1945 and 1950, he taught Korean Language, English Poetry, and Latin at Ewha Women's University, lectured on the Chinese *Book of Poetry* at Seoul National University, and worked for a Catholic publication, the *Kyŏnghyang Newspaper*. In 1950, Chŏng disappeared. It seems he was kidnapped and taken to the Communist north; so the publication of his poems in the southern part of Korea was banned until the end of 1987.

The revised edition of *The Collected Works of Chŏng Chi-yong, I: Poetry* (Seoul: Minŭmsa, July 1988) includes titles of 129 Korean poems together with several Japanese poems and Korean translations of Blake and Whitman. But taking into account two instances of several poems grouped together under one title and another two instances of approximate duplication of the same poem listed under different titles, the revised edition may be said to contain 139 original Korean poems. Of these, the present volume contains 115 English translations, chosen to display the variety of Chŏng's work at its best.

The Poetry of Chŏng Chi-Yong

Chŏng published his poems throughout a career that falls into three obvious divisions: the years of his study in Japan; those of his high-school teaching in Seoul; and the brief time between Korean liberation from Japan and the poet's disappearance. In the light of less obvious shifts in the focus and style of his poetry, however, it seems better to group his poems into the following four phases or periods:

I   1922(3)-1928, the student years: 54 poems;
II 1929-1935, the early teaching years: 47 poems;
III 1936-1942, subsequent teaching years: 29 poems;
IV 1945-1950, the years after liberation: 9 poems.

Often childlike and nostalgic, the poems of the first period express a fond attachment to one's home village and loved ones. Many also express a strong attraction for nature, especially for the sea, which often provides a setting for solitary musing. In the second period, ties of human affection give center stage to solitude; and the sea yields to the night sky as the most common backdrop for nostalgic solitude. In a handful of poems of this period, Christian images imbue the solitude with religious significance. In the third and last of Chŏng's main periods, the mountains that hover in the background of many earlier poems advance to the fore. We find whimsical verse vignettes of nature in the mountain sun and prose poems of life in the rugged solitude and mystery of the mountains at night. The slight output of the fourth period includes two patriotic poems and fresh treatments of the poet's persistent themes.

Chŏng manifests a poetic kinship with both modern western and traditional East Asian poets. He is a master of what Aristotle regards as the mark of poetic genius, metaphor (*Poetics*, 22.9); and he succeeds likewise in fulfilling the ideal espoused by traditional Chinese critics, a perfect fusion of feeling and landscape. With western readers in mind, I call attention especially to Chŏng's kinship with western poetic movements; but I do not mean to imply that he was specifically influenced by these movements. In any case, he draws upon a variety of poetic styles, east and west, but creates from them his own world and speaks with his own voice.

As the stylistic hallmark of his first period, personal feeling finds embodiment in scenes blended from realistic description, metaphors, and evocative Symbolist details, all reinforced by graceful rhythmic cadences. In such fashion, the speaker of the early poem "Nostalgia" recalls the countryside of his longed-for home village:

> The place where a rill, babbling old tales,
> Meanders on eastward toward the end of a broad plain
> And a mottled bull ox lows
> In dusk's plaintive tones of golden indolence—

Chŏng's first period also contains short verses reminiscent of the concision of Korean *sijo* and the naiveté of William Blake, as well as sprightly, freewheeling Imagist poems with a modern flair.

In the second period, Imagist poems grow in number; and pride of place belongs to a series of night poems in which the sinuous Realist-Symbolist cadences of the best early poems become more compact and chiseled in the Imagist manner. The first and second periods contain many of Chŏng's most memorable poems; but in one-fourth of the poems of these two periods—poems mostly excluded from the present translations—the imagery jars, the naiveté slips into banality, and the freewheeling structure gets out of kilter.

The third period has fewer poems and fewer slips. The tendency to compactness of imagery and phrasing continues in the mountain vignettes in verse. Less rich in emotional warmth than earlier poems, but charged with sudden sparks of wonder, these poems demonstrate the poet's skill with vivid, concise, evocative language at its best. The crown of his achievement, however, are the mountain prose poems, in which a compact, rustic style transmutes vivid Naturalism and playful, evocative fancy into a world of mountain magic.

Chŏng's musical sense and his facility with the variety of spoken Korean are just as keen as his powers of visual description and metaphorical inventiveness. He at times uses nursery-rime rhythms, sometimes fashions rhythmic prose poems, and most commonly creates a free verse whose rhythms are fitted to the particular demands of the situation. The poet's free use of onomatopoeia to reinforce his scenes provides a bane for the translator. Practically untranslatable, too, is the Korean countryside flavor that spices the diction. A problem for even a native reader is that, like Hopkins, Chŏng draws upon the full potential of his native language to achieve a vivid, down-to-earth quality. He freely uses out-of-date and dialectical forms; he relies on flexible spoken Korean usage rather than the set forms of modern grammar; and he feels free at times to fashion his own words in accord with their aural suggestiveness.

Another problem for the translator is how to convey the nuance of ambiguous expressions which, in accord with a typical Korean mode of discourse, assert something while at the same time qualifying, almost questioning the assertion. "A Bright Red Locomotive," for example, begins:

> In the idle moment of
>   a long, wandering gaze,
> Isn't love almost easy to understand!

Using not a special poetic device, but an ordinary Korean speech pattern, the second line in the Korean invites us to

consider a statement about love, but a tentative one; and the
tentativeness colors the tone of the whole poem. Ambiguity
of tone and imagery, elliptical structure, and a typically Ko-
rean ambiguity of discourse combine to create much of the
inner vitality of Chŏng's poetry. I have tried not to suppress
this vitality by translating away ambiguities.

The World of Human Ties

With an eye to chronological sequence, thematic focus,
and style, I have grouped the present translations under
eleven headings. The first three headings, *The Village of
One's Heart* and *Bonds of Affection I* and *II*, include poems
which focus on human ties. Clustering mainly in the student
years of Chŏng's first period (1922 to 1928), such poems con-
stitute one-half of the output of this period.

The *Chusŏk* Festival of early autumn sees millions of
Korean city dwellers headed for their ancestral homesteads in
the countryside to honor the dead at family graves and enjoy
together as a family the first fruits of harvest. Not just a place
to return to on holidays, the hometown has an archetypical
status in the Korean heart that makes it equivalent to a mythic
lost paradise. Away in Japan during his college years, Chŏng
must have felt an acute longing for his hometown; for several
poems of this period nostalgically romanticize scenes of Ko-
rean village life.

"Red Camellia Trees" (published in 1926) creates a real-
istic yet dreamy village scene from images that brim with the
contraries of rural existence: youth and age, nonchalance
and anxiety, affection and emptiness of heart, an endless
repetition of *yin* and *yang*. "Snatches of Old Tales" (1927)
expresses much the same feelings in a similar series of con-
trary images. In these poems, too, the young Chŏng no
doubt remembers his own hometown from the distance of
Japan; but he gives expression not just to private or purely
Korean feelings. He expresses emotions that could arise in
the unending cycle of rural village life anywhere.

The unambiguously titled "Nostalgia" (1927) was written shortly before or after Chŏng left Korea for study in Japan. It touches such deep common chords in the Korean heart that it managed to escape the full force of the proscription against the publication of Chŏng's poems after his disappearance in 1950. It has been set to music and is frequently heard sung on Korean radio. Simple in its overall structure, the poem consists of five balanced stanzas, each expressive of an aspect of the longed-for place of the speaker's youth and joined together by the refrain, "Could it ever be forgotten?" The appeal of the poem lies in the realistic yet imaginatively evocative scenes displayed in the gradually unfolding images of each stanza, scenes enlivened with naive wonder and spiced with rural dialect. Representative of the best of Chŏng's craft, these scenes are alive with a deep affection for life, fellow human beings, and nature. The poem provides a fine example of how a poem achieves universality by drawing upon the wellsprings of a particular people.

The Blakean parable "Hometown" (1932) appeared in the period after the poet's return to Korea. The speaker here makes explicit the archetypical character of the Korean longing for the village home when he says,

Home, I've come home;
But only the sky of my longing is a lofty blue!

The poems collected under the headings *Bonds of Affection I* and *II* give glimpses of the warm interaction between individuals that constitutes so much of the appeal of the village of the heart's longing. It has been said that the Korean heart is governed by *yang/yin* movements of *chŏng*, that is "affection," and *han*, the tangle of emotions that cloud a mind when affection darkens with frustration, regret, or bitterness. Chŏng Chi-yong's poems embody a *chŏng* that is seldom discolored by *han*. The affection of his poems is often tinged, however, by a Korean sensitivity to a threat of separation that fires affection to an even warmer glow.

"Little sister" and other childlike voices give utterance to the warmth of family ties and the poignancy of loss in a series of naive Blakean poems. "*Taekŭk* Fan" (1927) and two other poems of the same years deploy fuller cadences and richer images to express a parent's tender, awe-filled love for a child. "*Taekŭk* Fan" matches "Nostalgia" in its blend of Korean feeling and archetypical appeal and in its fusion of Realism and daydream fancy.

With "Dahlias" (1926) and "A Pomegranate" (1927), we leave childhood behind for bonds of affection that glow with sensuality and latent sexuality. "Dahlias" has a somewhat ambiguous, double focal point: flowers and a woman. The setting, too, pulls us in two directions. The setting embodied in the initial couplet arouses a sense of sensuous beauty:

A field of grass
Basking in the bright autumn sun.

But toward the end of the poem, the setting expands in a way that adds a sense of vast space and mystery:

Beneath a pond-like sky of
White water adrift with wild ducks.

As was mentioned above, the Chinese critical tradition has long espoused a poetic strategy of fusing feeling and natural scene. Under the influence of Taoism, moreover, Chinese poets since at least the third century have frequently adopted the poetic strategy of imbuing a scene with a sense of distance and space to enhance nature with an aura of wonder and mystery; and Korean poets have long followed suit. Under the influence of the French Symbolists, twentieth-century western poets have likewise made use of space to evoke a sense of mystery. In its quasi-mystic sensuousness, "Dahlias" bears as close a resemblance to poems of Mallarmé and Yeats as to traditional Asian poems; and "A Pomegranate," blurred in its focus and arcane in its allusion, shimmers with the wonder and sensuous beauty of a Symbolist poem.

At the opposite end of Chŏng's creative spectrum lies "The Mountain Lass and the Prairie Lad" (1926). Unique among Chŏng's poems, this poem takes us back to Medieval Korean *changga*, English ballads, and the ancient Chinese *Book of Poetry* that Chŏng lectured on in later life. Like such poems from older eras, this poem uses the simplest of images to dramatize a basic, instinctual human situation, in this case that of man hunting a woman. Part of the poem's appeal lies in the rural flavor of the language, which eludes translation.

Only six of the twenty-one poems included under the headings *Bonds of Affection I* and *II* are from periods later than the first. Four of these six later poems are miniature portraits. "Hands and a Candle Light" (1931) and "Red Hands" (1941) represent the invariably successful mode of many poems of the poet's third period: spare, rustic sketch. "Parasol" (1936) represents a style that Chŏng periodically adopts throughout his career, not always with success: whimsical pastiche.

The World of Nature and the Sea

As with most East Asian poets, Chŏng's imagination feeds on nature. Physical nature provides him with a store of metaphors and symbols; it almost always serves as the background or foreground of his settings; and at times it provides the center of his poetic focus, usually highlighted by playful whimsy and wonder.

Poems of the three categories *A Playful Eye on Nature, By the Sea,* and *Journeys and Crossings* exemplify styles seen in poems of village and personal ties. Many, too, have the same strong sense of human bonding. But they invite us first and foremost to savor contact with nature: spring birds, flowers, a horse, and especially the sea.

The three poems entitled "My Steed" form a little world of playful wonder and fellowship between man and animal. Miniature dramas of Imagist-Symbolist free verse, the two longer of these horse poems have also an affinity with the Korean folk narrative *p'ansori* in their comic vitality, musical word play, and free blend of realism and fancy.

All but one of Chŏng's poems focused on the sea come from the first two periods, and these sea poems constitute almost one-fourth of the total output of these periods. Heading the sea poems is "A Dream of Windblown Waves I" (1927). Written in 1922, this poem, along with "Nostalgia," represents Chŏng's earliest work. As in "Nostalgia," the poet marshals a series of long rhythmic cadences fashioned from evocative images alive with wonder and beauty. He summons up a seascape whose nostalgia encompasses a deep love of nature, a yearning for a beloved, and just pure, unfulfilled yearning. From the point of view of western poetry, the poem is Symbolist; but it does not indulge in the kind of aesthetic mysticism that French Symbolism is prone to. Its wonder and mystery are rooted in deeply felt contact with actual nature and a loved one. The haiku-like "Winter" (1930) and several other short sea poems likewise present the sea as a place of solitude, longing, and mystery, but in much simpler fashion.

"The Sea 1" (1927) and three later poems of "The Sea" series use what are basically Imagist techniques to give a taste of the physicality of the sea such as we find in early poems of Ezra Pound's *Cantos*. The best of these, "The Sea 6" (1930), demonstrates Chŏng's skill in controlling a flexible, elliptical structure and in wielding words and images to evoke physical sensation. The first half of the poem treats us to glimpses of a seascape that is free, clean, and vigorous in its beauty:

> Amid rock crannies fragrant with sea weed,
> Azalea-colored clams bask in the sun,
> While gliding blue terns wheel on their wings
> In the glasslike sky.

The second half becomes ambiguous and suggestive in the Symbolist manner. The poem ends up perhaps being not so much a sea poem as a love poem—depending on who or what the speaker is seen as addressing at the end. As "The Sea 6" unfolds, the seascape appears more and more in terms of typical Korean imagery: azaleas, flower-bud lanterns, pine, bamboo, and a whimsical tiger. Moreover, the poem achieves its evocative power by drawing on a typically Korean ambiguity of discourse; and as a love poem, it recalls the tradition of Korean love poetry which dwells on lovers' parting. Nonetheless, the experience evoked by the poem is universal.

On the whole, the sea poems have less of a traditional Korean air than poems centered on personal and village ties. Sea poems included under the heading *Journeys and Crossings* have a modern, foreign ring even when they portray something typically Korean. With results that are engaging but not profound, the poet plays with form, punctuation, and imagery in "A Sad Impressionist Painting" (1926) to create a kaleidoscopic impression of a modern seaside setting for the traditional Korean theme of departure. In "On the Deck" (1927), the poet at first uses modernistic images to evoke the excitement of a sea voyage and then juggles bits of imagery into place to form a modern illustration of a traditionally coy Korean encounter between the sexes.

Not all the poems of *Journeys and Crossings* involve a sea voyage. "A Melancholy Train" (1927) presents the interior monologue of a young man travelling by train along Japan's Inland Sea. The sea provides only a partial background, along with mountains, fields, and villages. As the scenes flow by, we feel the movement of the train; but we follow rather the vagaries of the speaker's heart, always with a Korean respect for the mystery of the human person. Molding the changing scenes from a combination of realistic detail and evocative connotation, Chŏng succeeds in presenting the enigmatic inner consciousness of a speaker whose moods shift from fanciful humor to passionate love and lighthearted

melancholy. In contrast with this poem, the interior mono-
logue of "A Train" (1932) embodies a more singly focused
melancholy in more compact form.

The World of Solitude

Many of the poems of Chŏng's first period and almost
one-half of those of the second breathe an air of nostalgic
solitude. We have found solitude in the village and solitude
by the sea. But we find, too, mainly in the second period
(1929-1935), numerous poems of nocturnal solitude and a
few poems of religious solitude. These poems are gathered
here under the headings *Nights' Solitude* and *The Christian
Imagination*.

The silken, dream monologue of "A Reed Flute" (1930)
evokes the magic and nostalgia of a lone moonlit night. The
compact, tangled night cry of "Window 1" (1930) expresses
the poet's personal turmoil at the death of his child. The
solitary speaker of this latter poem appears again and again
over the next twelve years, peering out from a window up at
the night sky, as the central figure of an extended theme and
variations. The variations culminate in a pair of contrasting
poems at the end of Chŏng's third period. The first of these,
the dreamy lullaby lyric "Stars 2" (1941), presents a longing
that finds fulfillment in the utter wonder of the night stars:

> Washed in cold water
> Spilling gold dust—
>   the silver currents of the Milky Way!

In contrast, "Window" (1942), the epitome of the lean, evoca-
tive style of the third period, expresses a longing for darkness
itself, a nocturnal darkness "lovely like vapor."

Appearing as they do at the height of the Japanese occu-
pation of Korea, these night poems may have social-historical
overtones. But just as the village poems draw their force from

realities that are archetypal rather than autobiographical, these poems draw their basic power from primal human realities rather than from reference to particular social or historical events.

One might expect the solitude of a poem from an East Asian country like Korea to reflect a Zen-like attitude of withdrawal from the turmoil of human feelings, and perhaps the preoccupation with darkness of the poem "Window" amounts to just such a withdrawal. But the poems of *Night's Solitude* as a whole are by no means detached Zen meditations. They are charged with longing, remorse, sorrow, passion, and wondrous intoxication.

When Chŏng invites his readers to religious meditation, it is rather in poems of *The Christian Imagination*, which were published mainly in 1933 and 1934. In his seven or eight Christian poems, the poet tosses images together in a way that does not represent him at his best. Still, in the simple parable of "The Sea of Galilee" (1933) and the mosaic of Biblical symbols that makes up "The Tree" (1934), Chŏng graces traditional Biblical and Catholic symbols with a provocative fancy not found in run-of-the-mill religious poetry.

The World of the Mountains

Two dozen of Chŏng's poems have a sea setting; many more are set at night; but still more are poems of the mountains. Chŏng finds his mature poetic voice as he settles lovingly into the solitude of night and the mountains. Two-thirds of the poems of his third period (1936-1942) are mountain poems, included here in the two categories *In the Mountains* and *The Prose Poems*. In these poems, the poet sets aside the earlier mask of a child, but still speaks with a child's fond fancy and loving wonder.

Traditional Chinese teaching has it that "A wise man loves the sea; a benevolent person loves the mountains." If so, the main tradition of Korean literature and painting as a whole favors benevolence; and Chŏng's poetry is no exception. Benevolent warmth pervaded the village poems and person-centered poems of his first period; it now transforms the rugged Korean settings of the mountain poems of the third period.

The verse poems of *In the Mountains* are gem-like mosaics of nature under the mountain sun. A few are more picturesque than profound; but in "Piro Peak 1" (1933) and "Okryu Valley" (1937), eye-catching description, inventive fancy, and enigmatic symbols crystalize in moments of mystical awe; and in "Piro Peak 2" (1938), "Kusŏng Valley" (1938), and "Rain" (1941), feeling and landscape fuse in a poetic alchemy rich in its yield of beauty, wonder, and exhilaration. A translator finds it quite a challenge to capture in English the concise ambiguity of the images of these verses and juggle them into place in a satisfying way.

In the case of the ten mountain prose poems, even Korean readers find a challenge. For the poetic ambiguity is compounded by rough syntax, rural dialect, archaisms, and the use of words that have not yet found their way into the dictionary. A western reader will be taken aback if he or she expects to find in these prose poems the stylized grace of a Tang Dynasty Chinese poem or a Korean *sijo.* Chŏng's mountain prose poems are the equal of his most graceful poems in freshness of fancy and depth of feeling; but they represent a Korean aesthetic tradition that seeks beauty, not in refinement and elegance, but in things commonplace and rough.

Appearing within the four-year span of 1938-1941, the mountain prose poems constitute a world all their own of Naturalism and fantasy, of rough, rugged beauty centered on life, love, and death in the mountains of winter or night. "Hot Springs" and "Pouch" (both 1938) project an ambiguously nuanced world in which feelings of solitude, fellowship, and warmth inside are cradled in the forbidding cold and soothing wonder of a winter night outside. The two "Changsu Mountain" poems (1939) display the loneliness and magic of a northern winter. The nine vignettes of "Paegnok Lake" (1939) evoke a gentler solitude and awe in the presence of the flowers, cattle, crater lake, and blue sky of Halla Mountain on the southern island of Cheju. "Bootleg Digging" and "Formal Attire" (both 1941) present fanciful parables of harsher realities.

Two long, subtly ironic love poems conclude *The Prose Poems.* One of these, "Melancholy Idol" (1938) is unique among Chŏng's poems. It is a whimsically erotic exploration of a woman's body, dignified by elevated linguistic forms traditionally reserved for religious ritual and the Korean court.

The Last Poems

The years between liberation from Japan in 1945 and Chŏng's disappearance in 1950 contain only nine poems. "You Return!" (1946) is included in the present collection as the better of two patriotic poems celebrating the end of Japanese domination. With its sometimes trite imagery, burdensome Chinese diction, march-like beat, and obvious emotion, it takes an about face from the general direction of Chŏng's work; but it gives forceful expression to feelings of the time. The very different poem "Untitled" (1949) is included because it appears to give testimony to Chŏng's poetic creed. On the whole rather enigmatic, it espouses poetry

That rough, coarse, and uncomely though it be,
Knows no falsehood, no rash assault.

More accurate and artistically more satisfying a testimony to Chŏng's career as a poet are a pair of contrasting encore pieces that echo his persistent themes in new ways. "Circus Troop" (February 1950) presents the musings of a man in his forties who has again become "a forlorn child" as he watches a circus. "Five Verses in Four-four Measure"

(June 1950) are terse transpositions of a traditional form, sparked by playful, childlike whimsy.

In determining which of Chŏng's poems to include in this volume and which to omit, I have consulted one of the most knowledgeable scholars of Chŏng's work, Professor Kim Hak-dong of Sogang University. But in the interest of balanced judgement, I should note that Professor Kim rates low the following poems that I regard highly and have decided to include: "Red Camellia Trees," "The Mountain Lass and the Prairie Lad," "A Bright Red Locomotive," "A Melancholy Train," "A Dream of Windblown Waves 1," "The Steed 2" (all from the first period) and the prose poem "Bootleg Digging" (third period).

The present translations are based on the revised edition of *The Collected Works of Chŏng Chi-yong, I: Poetry* (Seoul: Minŭmsa, July 1988), with reference to the originally published texts in a few doubtful instances. For help in preparing the translations, I am most grateful to Misters Kim Sŏng-whan, Shin Dong-ch'ŏl, and especially Cho Yong-hun. For assistance in checking them, I also thank Professors Kim Hak-dong, Chang Wang-rok, Kim Wook-dong, Lee Tae-dong, and Peter Fleming, as well as Misters Kim Yong-mun and Kim Yun-bae. I am also grateful to the Korean Culture and Arts Foundation, which has provided a generous subsidy for these translations and their publication, and to Chŏng Chi-yong's son, Mr. Chŏng Gu-gwan, who has graciously granted permission to publish the translations.

Following each poem is the date of publication along with the date of composition, when known, in parentheses.

The Village of One's Heart

HIDE AND SEEK

Shut my eyes and hide.
If you hug up close
        round the nut trees and pines,
I'll look high and low.

When all day long we play
        hide and seek,
I get sad.

Before I get sad,
I go and hunt blue birds.

Seeking again the countryside
        left long ago,
I go and hunt blue birds.

1927.2

RED CAMELLIA TREES[1]

Camellias are a blaze of blood-spewed crimson.
As a lazy spring day dips past noon,
The water mill turns without a care.

Children sing nonsense rimes to their dance,
And downy chicks cull feed in the sunlight.

On a village path where shimmering heat drowses,
Knowing, unknowing, in a weary daze,
I stroke my gaunt cheeks and return.

1926.11
(1924.4)

[1]Camillia: According to the dictionary, "chinaberry"; but the name of the tree given here is said also to refer to the camellia.

SNATCHES OF OLD TALES

On the paddy path
The night I was heading home,
I sang songs learned while away.

Setting out was hard,
And returning hard.
Setting out at fourteen had been hard.

I go on till cock-crow,
Telling father
The tales I'd gathered since leaving—

The oil lamp flickers and listens;
Tears welling up in her eyes,
    mother listens;
Dozing in her arms,
    my impish kid sister listens;
At a nearby doorpost,
    the wife stands and listens.

Like doleful water stored in huge jars,
The whispering country night
Turns with the villagers dropping in,
    to listen.

—But all are tales
Gathered from of old and enduring as ever
Beyond humble folk's power to halt.

The house-gate door pull, the roof,
Father's kindly old beard,
The night sky, bent like a bow,

All seem snatches of tales
Passed down from of old.

1927.1
(1925.4)

NOSTALGIA

The place where a rill, babbling old tales,
Meanders on eastward toward the end
    of a broad plain
And a mottled bull ox lows
In dusk's plaintive tones
    of golden indolence—

Could it ever be forgotten, even in one's dreams?

The place where ashes grow cold in a clay brazier
While over empty fields the sound of the night wind
    drives the horses
And our aged father, overcome with drowsiness,
Props his straw pillow—

Could it ever be forgotten, even in one's dreams?

The place where I got drenched
    in the rank weeds' dew,
Searching for an arrow recklessly shot
In the yearning of my earth-bred heart
For the sky's lustrous blue—

Could it ever be forgotten, even in one's dreams?

The place where little sister, dark earlocks
Flying like night waves dancing in a fairy-tale sea,
And my wife, not pretty but passable
    and all the year barefoot,
Bent their backs to the sun's tingling rays and
    gleaned ears of grain—

Could it ever be forgotten, even in one's dreams?

The place where sprinkled stars
    wend their way in the sky
Toward sand castles just beyond our ken,
While beneath drab roofs,
    hoary crows cawing past,
People sit, softly murmuring,
    round the faint firelight—

Could it ever be forgotten, even in one's dreams?

              1927.3
             (1923.3)

THE WOMEN OF OUR LAND

The women of our land are the May moon;
    they are joy.
Our womenfolk come out from the flowers,
    come out from sheaves of straw,
Bound out from the woods and waters.
Our women are red like mountain fruit,
The fragrance of *paduk* stones[1]
    gathered from the sea.
They are warm like sea currents.
Our women feed goats with green grass,
Water oxen at streams,
Breed mallard eggs, fine white eggs.
Our women embroider love birds.
They like to go barefoot; they're shy.
Our women part their mothers' hair,
Boast of their fathers' beards,
    are constantly teasing.
Our womenfolk relish raw chestnuts,
    walnuts, strawberries, potatoes.
Our women's elbows are round,
    their foreheads fair.
Their hair is the grass of spring,
    their shoulders the moon when full.

1928.5

[1]*Paduk* stones: the small black and white stone pieces used in the Korean chess-like game *paduk* (the Japanese *go*).

MEASLES

A December night silently withdraws
Around a primevally beautiful fire
That blooms in the coals.

No glow at the panes
And curtains drawn low,
Key set in the door,

A snowstorm buzzes and throbs
Like a swarm of bees;
And in a village, measles flourish
      like rhododendrons.

                                                1935.3

THE FAR SIDE OF THE MOUNTAIN

Who lives on the
Far side of the mountain?

All day in the hills,
Cuckoos call.

Who lives on the
Far side of the mountain?

Just the sound of hacking brush—
A harmonious jangle!

Who lives on the
Far side of the mountain?

As the spring sets in, no sign
Of even the usual pin peddler.

                                    1927.5

HOMETOWN

Home, I've come home,
But not to the home of my longing.

Wild pheasants brood eggs,
And cuckoos call in season,

But the heart doesn't have a hometown—
A cloud floating toward distant harbor.

Even today when I climb alone
    to the end of the mountain,
White-flecked flowers warmly smile,

While grass flutes blown in my youth
    yield no sound—
On parched lips, so bitter.

Home, I've come home;
But only the sky of my longing
    is a lofty blue!

1932.7

Bonds of Affection I

LITTLE SISTER AND THE PERSIMMONS

Yesterday a persimmon,
Today a persimmon.

Hey there, crow!
Why sit in our tree?

Big brother is coming.
Some are left for him to taste.

Clap, clap, clap—
Shoo, shoo!

1926.6

LITTLE SISTER AND THE SCARY CLOCK

In the room left by big brother,
The coals keep vigil like gourd blossoms.

Train rounding the mountain spur,
        voice hoarse—
Though not tonight, will it rain?

Again and again adjusting his cloak,
He'll be gazing out, won't he,
        on only black glass!

In the room left by big brother,
The clock sounds so eerie, I'm scared.

1932.1

LITTLE SISTER AND THE SETTING SUN

The place where big brother went—
He crossed the West Sea[1]
    where the sun goes down
And went, they say, far, far away.
Somehow I fear the sky there
More than the color of blood!
Has war broken out?
    Has a fire broken out?

                        1926.6

[1]The West Sea: the Yellow Sea.

GRAVE

I've come from burying little sister's grave
Fifteen *ri*[1] beyond the glen of the Village Spirit.
I've come from planting full blooming flowers
For birds round the house to hunt on an outing
When the yearly spring breezes come.

                        1935.10

[1]*Ri*: a Korean measure of distance, about four-tenths of a kilo-
meter.

LITTLE BROTHER AND THE BOTTLES

The night the owl was hooting,
Big sister's words—

If you break a blue bottle,
All at once, a blue sea;

If you break a red bottle,
All at once, a red sea.

The day the cuckoo was calling,
My big sister married—

Smashing a blue bottle,
I gaze alone at the sky;

Smashing a red bottle,
I gaze alone at the sky.

1926.6

PLAY DOLL

Dolly and Little Auntie—
Always comrades, we three,
Beneath the cherry tree.

Dolly blundered
And went blind.

I returned after
        seeking blind Dolly,
And someone had run off
With Little Auntie too.

Alone, I shake a bell.
Disgusted, I cry.

                                        1926.6

GRANDFATHER

When grandpa
Sticks his pipe in his mouth
And goes out into the fields,
Even a bad day
Beautifully clears.

When grandpa
Puts on his straw rain cape
And goes out into the fields,
Even a day in a dry spell
Has rain.

                                        1927.5

THE THIRD DAY OF THE THIRD MONTH[1]

Monk, monk, a boy monk—
Close-cropped hair, our little baby![2]

The third of March,
Butterflies, flit, flit;
Baby swallows, flit, flit.

We picked mugwort
To flavor crescent rice cakes.[3]
Whiff, whiff, cooled them off;
Yum-yum, tasted good!

Monk, monk, a boy monk—
Buy our baby for a disciple.

1926.6

[1]The third day of the third month by the lunar calendar, or sometime in April by the solar calendar. On this festive day, married women traditionally bathe for purification; swallows return; and butterflies appear. People would read their fortunes in the butterflies, taking yellow swallowtails as a sign that their wishes would be fulfilled and white butterflies as a sign that a parent would die.

[2]Mothers recite this in play with little children; they also recite the nonsense verse of lines four and five, while making flapping arm gestures.

[3]Crescent rice cakes: *Kaep'i* rice cakes, that is bite-sized rice cakes shaped like a half-moon and filled with bean-paste. When flavored with mugwort, they are green.

T'AEKŬK FAN[1]

Maybe the child is chasing a rubber ball,
Coursing over green grass where
      white mountain goats call to one another.

Longing after a swallowtail butterfly,
Maybe the child is dashing along the edge of
      a breath-taking cliff.

All at once sprouting wings,
Maybe he is circling about a sky
      where flower-dragonflies[2] hold fair.

      The child is surely not
            lying on my knees.

He's commanding troops of birds and flowers,
      dolls, tin soldiers, locomotives—
Going around like a long-legged prince
Between the sand and the sea,
      the moon and the stars.

      I've had my days by a stream
            flowing till dusk,
      Just stripping straw flutes
      Out of unsought anxiety
            for this child.

Note the sound of the child's
      silk-waved breathing,
His brave, tender air;
The pumpkin-flower smile
      that dwells on his lips.

I'm suddenly taken up with
Accounts, rice, a leaky roof.

On a night when fireflies faintly flit
And earth worms weep enough for an oil-lamp,
The handle of a *t'aegŭk* fan with hardly a sorrow
Flutters in the gathering hot breeze.

1927.8
(1927.6)

[1] *Taekŭk* fan: fan marked with the Chinese symbol of the cosmos seen on the Korean national flag.

[2] Flower-dragonflies: an expression used for pretty dragonflies. Korean children like to catch dragonflies.

A BRIGHT RED LOCOMOTIVE

In the idle moment of
      a long, wandering gaze,
Isn't love almost easy to understand!
Come on, little tot, run!
If the fire rising so fair in your cheeks
Should fade too soon, what would we do?
Come on, scoot along!
Whee— Whee— the wind!
As if floating up, body and all,
      on the hem of a cloak.
Aswirl, aswirl, the snow!
Like feed luring the fry of carp.
Come on, little tot,
Like a red locomotive,
      bright and unknowing,
            run!

                              1927.2
                              (1925.1)

AN ATTACK OF FEVER

On a night when grape shoots creep out
Toward smoke hanging at the eaves, all still,
Hot vapors seeping through
    the drought-torn soil
Rise at the back, warm.
Ah, again, how the child's body burns!
As its breathing heaves mothlike,
I press my lips to the injection mark
    on the frail head
And mutter, I mutter
Like an unabashed polytheist.
Ah, the child piteously whines!
On a night with no fire,
    no medicine, no moon,
In the far-off sky
Stars seem to sail like bees.

1927.7
(1927.6)

Bonds of Affection II

DAHLIAS

A field of grass
Basking in the bright autumn sun—

Dahlias in full bloom,
Fully bloomed dahlias at noon.

The fresh luster of your flesh
Is also ripe as can be;

Your breasts and coyness,
Ripe as ripe can be.

Be gentle, I beg you;
Gambol like a doe.

Beneath a pond-like sky of
White water adrift with wild ducks,

Full blooming dahlias—
Dahlias not blooming,
    but bursting in bloom.

                                    1926.11
                                    (1924.11)

A POMEGRANATE

Brazier coals blooming to a
       lovely rose-like blaze—
Dry grass kindled on the First Day of Spring[1]
       scents the night.

When I split a pomegranate
       that got past the dead of winter
And taste, one by one, the ruby-like beads,

Diaphanous thoughts of old,
       rainbows of new cares,
Goldfish-like, tender, childlike sensations!

The fruit must have ripened last lunar October,[2]
When the little story of the two of us began.

Little Miss, slender comrade,
A pair of jade rabbits[3] secretly nestling,
       drowsing at your breast.

Fingers, white-fish fingers
       swimming in an ancient pond,
Threads, silver threads,
       fluttering freely, lonely, and light—

Holding to the light
       bead after bead of pomegranate seed,
Dreaming of Shilla's[4] thousand years of blue sky.

                                           1927.3
                                          (1924.2)

[1]The First Day of Spring: around February 4, the first of twenty-four calendar divisions marked by the height of the sun.

[2]Lunar October: by the solar calendar, November.

[3]Jade rabbits: According to Korean legend, a jade rabbit lives on the moon.

[4]Shilla: the historically important and culturally rich kingdom that dominated the Korean peninsula from the seventh to the tenth century.

THE MOUNTAIN LASS AND THE PRAIRIE LAD

For mountain birds, to the mountains;
For prairie birds, to the plains.
Let's go to the mountains
To catch a mountain lass.

Crossing a low pass,
Climbing a tall peak—

"Jo-ho!"[1]
"Jo-ho!"

A mountain lass is
Nimble like a leopard.

As she scampered away,
The mountain lass,
You snagged her with an arrow,
        did you?

Not at all.
When this prairie lad
        caught hold of her hand,
She would hardly let go.

Once the mountain lass
Was fed prairie rice,
She forgot, she did,
        the language of the mountains.

As night came on
In the yard on the prairie

If one took a peek
Beyond the blazing bonfire—

At the sound of the prairie lad's
    wily laugh,
The face of the mountain lass
    was a rush of scarlet.

1926.11
(1924.4.22)

WHAT WILL ANYONE SAY?

Take the main road,
Cross a ridge, and there's our house.
Avoid the front gate;
Come by the path
    through the hills out back.
On a late spring day
When misty rain falls
    a soft peach-blossom pink,
Come by the path
    through the hills out back.
If you drop by as if in from the wind,
What will anyone say?

1927.2

[1] A common mountain call, intoned slowly with full voice.

HANDS AND A CANDLE LIGHT

A match lit with quiet skill,
The flame filling the room!

In a wink, as if nestled
        in a bunch of flowers,
It rises like an owl,
        eyes wide open.

Your ruddy hands
Draw water from rock crannies,
Pour mountain-goats' milk,
Raise plain vegetables.
Like a rose blossoming
On a mystic branch,
At your hands the night-light
        gives birth.

                                        1931.11

RED HANDS

Shoulders round,
Lush hair-braid trailing,
Bred in the mountains,
Forehead white as an egg.

In black padded socks[1]
   patched white at heel and toe,
Hands frozen red like mountain berries,
She plows through a path of snow
To draw water tapped from stone crannies.

As a strand of blue smoke rises,
The roof glows warm in the sunshine;
And again, in the snow,
The virgin gives off the fresh green scent
   of midway up a parasol tree.[2]

Sitting bashfully turned,
   an out-of-season wayfarer,
She casts the image of her face
   in the gathering steam
And takes a peek at spring water
   that in between the stones
     is strangely like the sky.

                    1941.1

[1]Padded socks: Korean *pŏsŏn*. Black *pŏsŏn* were formerly worn by the lower class.
[2]The bark of the parasol tree has a green color even when old.

FLOWERS AND A FRIEND

Many a tight squeeze
Where the rock wall is sheer—
All day long edging around,
And again it's touch and go!

My friend was clutching at rocks
And stopping for breath
Every seven steps.

Picking wild flowers,
I was busy, rather,
Adorning my hair and lapel.

I decked myself out in red flowers
        like an aboriginal
And took all the more pleasure
        on the trail behind my friend,
His dignity regained for all his frailty.

At a spot where birdcalls ceased,
I saw autumn's lush hues
In the tail of a chipmunk wheeling
        around upright on a white stone brow.

As if close by, waterfalls rumbled;
And my friend's call was
All the more melodious,
Returned in the resounding echo.

Dodging sheets
Of a flash attack of rain,
We found a cave abandoned by beasts
And, shivering, discussed our hunger.

No sooner did distant waters rise,
Scowling dark blue beyond
    white-birch branches,
Than, red like a ground cherry,
    the sun got swamped.

Where the path breaks off
Between stars and flowers,
We now light a fire and lie down.

All rumpled
In a camel-hair coat,
My friend falls asleep on the spot,
    like a butterfly.

We've climbed above the clouds;
And my friend, seized with weariness,
Is all the more pretty, like a wife.
So I don't mind keeping guard, wide awake.

                    1941.1

MY TYPE OF PERSON

You're my type of person.
As handsome goes, a bit undersized;
But feign an air of silly bewilderment
And show a winning smile
    like people in the good old days.
Turn this way, please;
    now that way, please.
Take hold of your nose,
    turn round and round, and
        be so kind as to take just one bow.

Ho, ho, ho, my type of person!

Mounted on a huge steed,
If you should gallop out
Toward plains spanned by
    a double rainbow arch,

I'd sit on a grassy peak
And call commands:

"Forward— march!"
"About face— march!"

Slim and trim,
    shoulders like mountain tops.
Ho, ho, ho, my type of person!

                  1927.2
                (1924.10)

WORDS ON A POSTCARD

Pretend it's a butterfly flown your way
And turn the light on this sheet of paper.
It will flutter a while on its own.
        —A little like a paltry bit of life.
One of your timid brothers, though,
Forges through fire far and near
And, drenched with cold rain, has come.
        —A little like a not-so-dreary tale.
Sleep, sister, like the fair Muse
Till this black night is all white.
Down from a thousand-foot peak,
Comes now the wind.

                                                    1927.5
                                                    (1927.3)

PARASOL

As lotus leaves give off a lotus scent,
She gives off a lotus-leaf fragrance.

Transplanted across sea straits,
She'd still be green, just as straits are green.

Cheeks that blush without warning are a
    nuisance,
Just as flowers of themselves, a torment.

She doesn't let tears gather long.
At the rotary press, she's busy as an angel.

Careful all her life to choose not just red roses,
For a gift she usually gives lilies.

She rushed into a lake that's simply too full;
But somehow or other, she forges ahead.

For the last act of a variety show,
She carouses like a desperate swan.

Though shy, a good eater—
Like even a horrendous steak!

Slack as a spring
From office fatigue,

She's covered the lamp
And right off locked the door.

There's no knowing her prayer or her sleep;
In a roaring black night, she's white as an egg.

She hates
Getting wrinkled or soaked;

Neatly folded like a parasol,
Always, like a parasol, ready to unfold—

1936.6

A Playful Eye on Nature

BIRD FROM THE MOUNTAIN

On the wall sprouting with dodder vines,
There calls a bird from the mountain.

Bird from the mountain, skirted in blue;
Bird from the mountain, capped in red.

The bird longs for a look at what haunts its eyes,
A look at kid sister, gone away barefoot.

From early morning this warm spring day,
Calls the bird from the mountain.

1927.6

THE SKYLARK

At me, stepping out from a long winter freeze—
Warbling, warbling . . . . a skylark.

Why does he go on poking fun like that?

At me, raised motherless—
Warbling, warbling . . . . the skylark.

Why does he go on poking fun?

All day long this bright spring day,
I'll just play alone on the sand flats.

                                        1935.10

SPRING

Beneath where a lone crow cawed and took flight,
Stand four dilapidated stone pillars.
Traces of moss still green,
The twilight glows crimson.

As the wind moves along the water,
A bridge formed by a rising turtle's back,
A quite long bridge,
Is, swish, swept aslant.

                                        1932.4

ORCHIDS

Orchid leaves,
The color, rather,
    of pale black ink.

Over orchid leaves
Come dreams and fine mist.

Orchid leaves
Have lips closed—
    open in the dead of night.

Orchid leaves
Open eyes in starlight
    and again lie down.

Orchid leaves
Can't help their bare elbows.

Over the orchid leaves
Comes a light breeze.

The orchid leaves
Are cold.

1932.1

THE STEED 1

Steed, towering steed,
Though genteel,
Why so sad?
Steed, trusty steed,
Look what I've got for you—
      beans, black and green.

This horse is a motherless child.
Comes night, and it falls asleep
      gazing at the faraway moon.

                                        1927.7

THE STEED 2

At bamboo roots, heave! I've landed on my rump,
      tearing them out.
Steeped in the tide, I flail—swish, swish—and the
      purple-blooming sky gently billows.
Before the whip, the sea wails;
Above the sea, gulls scatter.

I've sought out my brother steed, who assumes a
      wistful, drowsy air in the shade of the paulownia trees.
"It's a lovely morning, brother."
In my steed's eyes, yesterday evening's new spring moon
      rolls hazily round.
"Lay your cheeks this way, brother. Hey! Clang, bang!"

Before the steed's white teeth, the sea tingles;
On hills dyed green, sunbeams glisten like mother-of-pearl.
"On such a radiant day, brother, love is a trifle."

The sea comes, folding fine skirt pleats.
"I've bound up bashful spots, brother,
So snort away."

Clouds spread out with a marble sheen;
The whiplash flashes the sketch of a snake.
"Heigh! Heigh! Heigh! Heigh! Heigh! Heigh!"

The steed's forelegs are hind legs; hind legs, forelegs.
At the ears swirls the sea.
Swish! Swish! Swish!
Eight legs, sixteen!
The sea comes barking like a pack of wolves.

Swish! Swish! Swish!
Sweeping past my shoulders, the head wind whistles.
Over land and sea, August flutters.

"Brother, o-oh my long-tailed hero!"
On such a radiant day, a wavy mane is a thing of pride![1]

1927.9

[1]The Korean text actually closes the quotation at the end of both of the last two lines. Which close the author intended is a guess.

THE STEED 3

Magpies fly ahead,
The horse follows.
Breezes murmuring, water purling,
The June sky round, ahead a vast plain—
Everywhere you look, our land!
Ah, so good to go bare-chested, so good to
        whistle!
The whip twirls, twirls, twirls, twirls!
Horse,
Who bore you? You. You don't know!
Horse,
Who bore me? Me, too. I don't know!
You live in the backwoods,
Hiding your manlike breathing;
I've grown up in the heart of the city,
Hiding my horselike breathing.
No matter where, country or city,
It's been sad without parents.
Neigh, horse,
To make the echoes jangle!
I'll add my voice to the sad brass-bell sound.[1]
The sun at mid-sky, golden sunflowers turn,
While the far white sea breaks above field ridges
Swaying with blossoming bean hedges.
Horse.
Let's go. Go, I say! Out on a
        wayfarer's road of old.
The horse goes,
The magpies follow.

                                        1935.10

[1]Perhaps this line refers to both the neighing echo and the
brass bell that customarily hung from a horse's neck.

SUNFLOWER SEEDS

Let's plant sunflower seeds.
Out of sight of the sparrows
  at the crook in the wall,
Let's plant sunflower seeds.

When big sister pats them down
  with her hands,
Pooch pats them down with his paws
And puss with her tail.

When we close our eyes
  and sleep the night through,
Dew settles, sleeps together, and goes.

While we're off at the neighbors,
The sun's rays give a kiss and go.

A sunflower is a new bride.
After three days still bashful,
She never lifts her head.

That fellow who came
  to steal a still look
And left with a shriek!—
Oh, it's that rascal of a tree frog
Hidden in the leaves of the spindle tree.[1]

          1927.6

[1]Spindle tree: a kind of shrublike evergreen.

AN EARLY SPRING MORNING

The warbling of a strange bird reaches my ear;
And pelted and pummelled by a pretty silver clock,
My heart splits this way and that with care
And swirls round and round like a glob of mercury—
I'm chilly and sure hate getting up.

Ever so gently, as if to grab a mouse,
When I sli—de open the door and take a look,
In the breeze with just my shorts, oh! it's freezing!

Between withered dodder vines,
A fledgling mountain red-bird goes in and out
        like a spinning-wheel shuttle.

Though it's just a baby bird,
        I feel I can trade a word or two.
Its keen, tender heart is all aflutter.
The Esperanto we use, the baby bird and I,
        is all whistles.
Hey, little bird, don't fly away; sing all day long.
I'm as lonely this morning as a baby elephant.

The mountain peak, formed there in profile,
Is tinged with the color of pinks.
Like a briskly rising marble column,
Cut smooth and set in place,
It sustains with all its might
A morning sky ablaze with a liver-like sun.
Swishing round the waist like a sash,
A spring breeze sails in with a rustle;
And the little bird blows in with a whirr!

1927.2

By the Sea

A DREAM OF WINDBLOWN WAVES 1

You say you are coming—
Just how will you come?

Like the grape-dark night surging in
To the sound of an endless cry
    that embraces the sea—
Is that how you'll come?

You say you are coming—
Just how will you come?

Like an ashen silver giant from
    a forlorn isle across the sea,
Swooping down on a day fierce with wind—
Is that how you'll come?

You say you are coming—
Just how will you come?

When outside the window
    sparrows' eyes droop
And inside, chin in hands,
    I'm crushed with care . . . .
Like the dawn moon, round like
    a silver door pull,
Doffing a veil tinged with shame—
Is that how you'll come?

When a spell of lonely slumber
        haunts windblown waves,
The front harbor lies wrapped
        in a bank of foul rain;
And from a passing boat a drum beat sounds,
        a drum beat sounds.

                                        1927.7
                                       (1922.3)

A DREAM OF WINDBLOWN WAVES 2

Though the wind blows fierce,
The moon, timeless lamp,
Inextinguishable!
At dusk, my love was stowed aboard
        and sent over windblown waves.
In the dead of night, I awake,
        startled by a frightening dream.

                                        1931.10

THE SEA 1

Oh · Oh · Oh · rushing out with a shout,
Oh · Oh · Oh · again and again, surging in.

In last night's slumber, soft,
Far-off thunder rumbled;

And the morning sea
Is swollen the color of grapes.

Plashing, splashing, lapping—
The waves dance in and about
    like flying swallows.

                  1927.2
               (1926.1)

THE SEA 2

As if out from a century
Hid in the mud,

I sidle along crablike
And take a look—

Beneath distant blue skies,
An endless stretch of sand.

                  1927.2
               (1926.1)

THE SEA 3

A lonely soul
All day long

Calls to the sea—

Over the sea
Night
Comes walking.

                              1927.2
                              (1926.1)

THE SEA 4

The limp sound of waves to my back,
    I turn away alone,
When out of nowhere—
        one sunk to the ground?—
            a moan!

When I turn and look,
    a far-off beacon flashes;
And a flock of gulls fly on,
        squalling, squalling,
            calling the rain.

The one moaning is neither
        beacon nor gull—
The nameless sorrow, somewhere,
        of one fallen alone.

                              1927.2
                              (1926.1)

THE SEA 5

A *paduk* stone[1]—
To be fondled in my palm
Must sure feel good.

But I've pitched it, I have,
Into the deep blue sea.

A *paduk* stone—
To fall headlong into the sea
Must sure feel marvelous.

You, too, now,
Stop fondling me.
Take me by the ear and cast me away.

I, too, what's called "I"—
To fall headlong into the sea—
How refreshing!

The *paduk* stone's heart
And these thoughts of mine
Are known to no one.

1927.3
(1925.4)

[1]*Paduk* stones are the small black and white stone pieces used
in the Korean chesslike game *paduk* (the Japanese *go*).

THE SEA 6

A whale has cut across,
And the channel now flaps like a tent.

.... *Paduk* stones settling, settling
        beneath blossoming white waves.

Soaring sea larks, like beads of
        molten silver flown aloft . . . .

Peering down the whole day long,
        they seek to clutch and snatch
                crimson flesh.

Amid rock crannies fragrant with sea weed,
Azalea-colored clams bask in the sun,
While gliding blue terns
        wheel on their wings
In the glasslike sky.
The sea, disclosed
        to its depths.
A sea's
Bamboo-green
Spring

What does it seem?
—Hills aglow with
Strands of flower-bud lanterns?

—Woods luxuriant with
Pine and bamboo?

—A crouched tiger, wrapped in a
Yellow and black mottled blanket?

Accompanied by seascapes of spring,
Sail the white-smoke sea
Far, far away.

1930.5

THE SEA 7

Blue,
The sea;
White, so white,
The sand.
On the horizon
A softly subsiding
Noon sky,
The sun revolving at dead center.
My soul, too,
Now tranquilly spins
A white-gold top on the verge of tears.

1930.9

THE SEA 8

White clouds
Blossom;
The scented winds
Are full.
Seaweed abounds;
Shellfish get plump;
And ah! the tangy sea—
Like essence of ginger.
Spying now a
Blade-like shark,
We rush to the bow.
In tatters, the red sail flutters.
The arm's full thrust!
Spear-tip right on!

1930.9

THE SEA 9

Helter-skelter,
The sea sought flight.

Lickety-split
Like a bunch of green lizards—

No way to
Grab the tails.

Scratches torn by white claws,
More crimson and pathetic than coral!

Barely managing a massed surge,
It trims round the rim
        and skims off moisture,

Plucking rinsed hands
From this Elsin[1] marine chart.

Till, brimming, it spills
And tumbling, rolls,

It swirls up in offering.
Like lotus petals,
        the earth's globe folds . . . .
                and unfolds . . . .

1935.12

[1]Elsin: Perhaps, as has been suggested, the poet invented this name to give the poem a western flavor.

SEA GULLS

Though I turn and look, not a hill. Not a pine or blade of
    grass.
The sun seethes at mid-sky like a white-gold crucible; the
    round sea spins like a top.
Gulls, gulls, you sound like cats.
Cats living here? Where were you born? Throats so white,
    wings white, claws so trim, you snatch bounding fish.
Gulls, gulls, did you spring up unawares,
White waves breaking, blue water-whorls settling?
Me, I was born by the light of an oil lamp, while black night
    rain cried on the porch stone.
I've a mother, a father. Their hair is all white.
I'm a trim, slender youth, with one I alone have pined for,
    left in a village where jujube trees bloom.
Gulls, gulls, you coil the waves round your neck, thrust
    with your claws.
Into the water, shooting out, whirling; veering, you soar.
Can you live without rice? My hands swell so![1]
Strange clouds on the horizon, strange winds in the sail.
Arms folded, eyes closed, I caress the sea's loneliness
        like a black necktie.

                                           1928.9
                                          (1927.8)

[1]Perhaps the speaker means that his hands swell if he does not
eat enough.

LAKE SURFACE

The sound of a handclap
Cuts beautifully across.

In its trail, white geese glide.

1927.2

LAKE 2

A mallard's neck
Coils the lake.

A mallard's neck
Constantly tickles.

1930.5

WINTER

Raindrops fall, roll along in beads of hail,
And in the dead of night
    are borne across an ink-black sea.

1930.1

Journeys and Crossings

A SAD IMPRESSIONIST PAINTING

On an early summer evening
Bearing the scent of watermelon . . . . . .

Lamps. Electric lamps,
Lined up in trees along the road
Toward the distant seashore—
Gleaming, glistening, as if out from a swim!

Whistles . . . . Steam whistles . . . .
Resounding dismally from the harbor works.
Flags. Customshouse flags,
Fluttering with an exotic flair.

A touch of white western finery
Tripping lightly along the sidewalk!

A fleeting, cheerless sight . . . .
The anxiety of idly chewing an orange peel . . . .

Oh, Mr. Aesiri Whang![1]
You're headed for Shanghai[2] . . . . . .

1926.6

[1]Aesiri Whang: The name suggests a Korean living in Japan.
[2]Shanghai was the base of the Korean Independence Movement under Japanese occupation. Perhaps the poem reflects this.

THE FRUIT OF THE CHERRY TREE

That cherry on your upper lip—has it healed?
Has that cherry vanished, then, as if all blotted out?
Ever since you went off, buzzing like a bee, three
    nights ago,
The firelight wears a halo as of sprinkled pine pollen.
In paper weather-strips, quiver dim distant rapids of
    melted ice.
With the wind slithering in with such force these days,
Even sinews and joints in their prime easily go bad.
The time's getting near to set out for lonely Kangwha
    Island.[1]
That cherry on your upper lip—what if doesn't heal?
Will you let it just dangle, then, and go?

1927.5
(1927.3)

[1]Kangwha Island: off the West Coast of Korea at the mouth of
the Imjin River.

ABOVE DECK

The low-hanging sky gleams white gold,
And seething waves shatter like sheets of glass.
In the rolling salt winds, distilled blood teems at every
    cheek,
While the ship barks like a splendid beast and dashes on.
A lone island that suddenly blocks our passage like a black
    pirate
Retreats shilly-shally behind the wings of scattering gulls.
Nestled in the crook of huge white arms everywhere I look,
The globe's round mass is a joy.
My necktie flies briskly; June's rays soak shoulders back to
    back;
My endlessly stretching gaze flutters, flag-like, out to the
    horizon.

The sea winds flicker in her hair!
Her hair, as if sorrowful, quivers.

The sea winds play pranks with her skirt!
Her skirt, as if bashful, flutters.

She looks at the winds and scolds them.

A sudden plunge on a lark would hardly mean death!
Ever teasing the sea with banana peels,

Looking down in unison and lightly laughing
Before swirling eddies that snarl our young hearts.

                             1927.1
                       (1926 summer)

A MELANCHOLY TRAIN

Puffing on a waggish seaman's pipe, our train chugs
    along the whole spring day of an island nation
        shimmering with heat.
Like a lazily lumbering June cow, our train ambles along.

Gasping and panting between high sloping fields of yellow
    cabbage,
The train chugs along.

Though always a bit sad, I'm light of heart.
At my ease against the window, I'll just let fly a whistle.

A distant mountain comes charging like cavalry horse;
    a nearby forest blows away like the wind.
Spread out like a sheet of glass, the Inland Sea's[1] vast
    water, water, water—
Dip in your hand, and it would turn the color of grapes.

Wet your lips, and they would boil like soda.
Embracing the wind in plump sails, a motley of boats toss
    about like tops,
Then turn into butterflies and fly away.

At my ease against the train window, I'll just slip into
    blissful slumber like the jade hare.[2]
In the collar of her blue mantle, Madame R's worn cheeks
    bloom a reddish tint, flicker like a lovely coal fire.
What does it mean, her singing an absurd child's lullaby?

           Go to sleep,
           My poor little boy;
           Go to sleep.

I'm not her little boy! With this beard coming on, not a boy
    for some time now!
Projecting listless puffs of breath on the window, I'll just
    draw my favorite name and travel on.
I'll wash down my heartburn with chunks of tangerine.

At wall after wall of bamboo thicket, blood-red camellia[3]
    trees ooze with voluptuous desire.
In yard after yard, the soft fluff of downy chicks;
At every roof, smokeless sunbeams blaze.
Such clear skies! My head spins, a spinning like love!

In the collar of her blue mantle, Madame R's pitiable lips
    all the while tremble.
Sisterly lips! This day I bow before them in heartfelt
    recompense.
Though always a bit sad of heart,
O-oh, I've no desire to fly faster than the train.

1927.5

[1]The Inland Sea of Japan.
[2]According to Korean legend, a hare as lovely as jade lives on
the moon.
[3]Camellia: According to the dictionary, "chinaberry"; but china-
berry trees have white flowers. I am told that the name of the tree
given here is also used to refer to the camellia.

A TRAIN

Grandma,
What's so sad that makes you cry?
Crying, crying, headed for Kagoshima.[1]

A kerchief of tattered homespun
Drenched with tears.
No! though I lean this way and that,
Haunted by memories,
I never shall sleep.

I, too—my teeth ache
To seek my home town.

The train travels
An April breeze yellow with cabbage flowers.
Teeth clenched, it rushes on.

                                                1932.7

[1]Kagoshima: a city at the southern end of Japan.

MAY NEWS

Don't you long for our early summer,
    fire-bright with Paulownia blossoms?
For a tender wayfarer's dreams may at times
    turn into a bluebird.
Beneath a tree, or head on my desk,
There whisper at my ears only the
    memories you left behind.

My glad heart quickens as the
    long-awaited news flies in;
In every heart-rending pen stroke
    surges the far Yellow Sea.

. . . . I'm urging to the utmost
    my little gull-like boat . . . .

Might not a sprightly May necktie turn
    straight away into a sudden fair wind
And go seek the romance of a faraway isle
That shoots above blue waves rising
    right against the sky?

This little Pestalozzi, my oriole-like teacher,
Gone off to teach Arabic letters[1] and Japanese!
The island rim seems gnawed night and day by
    anxious wind-blown waves—
The sound of an organ, as in a muffled surge,
    wailing in the distance . . . . . .

                  1927.6

[1]Presumably the poet means Arabic numerals.

SEA STRAITS

At a porthole bored round as if by a shell,
Peeps a horizon bulging to the eyebrows,

While the sky, easing down,
Broods like a huge hen.

My spot, lone and free!
Where schools of crystalline fish parade.

An ear rising at a mantle collar
Sounds, conch-like, the bugle
        of a tumultuous desert isle.

The straits' solitude at two in the morning
        wears a flawless halo.
I'll just well up, like a girl, with idle tears.

My youth is my fatherland!
The clear skies of tomorrow's harbor!

The voyage seethes just like love,
And somewhere now blooms a midnight sun.

                                        1933.6

AGAIN THE SEA STRAITS

The sea straits near noon—
A sharp circumference traced in chalk!

Red masthead flag
    more beautiful than the sky.
Sea furrows surging lush—
    bunch upon bunch of cabbage!

Like dappled horses, like seals,
    lovely islands rush up,
Only to pass one by one without contact.

The sea straits wobble like a
    toppling water-mirror.
The straits don't spill.

Does creeping up over the globe
Cause such a flutter!

When we pass an out-of-the-way place,
    the whistle cries in fright,
Plaintive like a donkey!

July sunshine on the straits,
More refreshing than moonlight!

Side by side at the smoke-stack ladder,
I and a chap speaking Cheju[1] dialect
    have become good friends—

At age twenty-one on the first crossing,
Learning cigarettes before love.

1935.8

[1]Cheju: the island province at the southern tip of Korea.

Night's Solitude

KAMOGAWA[1]

On Kamogawa's ten-*ri*[2] plain,
The sun sinks to dusk . . . .
    down to dusk . . . .

Day in, day out,
    the one I love sent away,
My throat has gone dry . . . .
    the sound of shoals . . . .

A cold heart wringing moisture
    from cold grains of sand,
Squeeze! Grind! How futile!

From her nest of thick knotweed,
A marsh hen lets out a widow's cry,

While a pair of swallows rise,
Dancing to greet the rain.

An evening stream breeze
    bearing the scent of watermelon.
Cares of a wayfaring youth
    chewing on an orange peel.

On Kamogawa's ten-*ri* plain,
The sun sinks to dusk . . . .
    down to dusk . . . .

1927.6

[1]Kamogawa: Mallard Brook, the name of the Japanese city in the vicinity of Tokyo where Chŏng Chi-yong lived for a time.

[2]*Ri*: a Korean measure of distance, about four-tenths of a kilometer.

A REED FLUTE

Can you catch a mermaid
And make her your wife?

On a night like this,
         the moon so wan,
Roaming the sea's warm depths . . . .

Can you become a glasslike ghost
And appear just bare bones?

On a night like this,
         the moon so wan,
Riding a balloon
And floating, floating
         toward a pollen-strewn sky . . . .

In a tree's empty shade,
I converse with my flute,
         just we two together.

                                        1930.5

NIGHT

Through snow-laden clouds
Flows a white moon.

Gathered at the eaves,
        flow brier-orange trees.

A lone candle's flame,
        a water bird's nest,
                flowing . . . .

Wrapped lonely in a leopard skin,
I lie down and cross tonight's
        desolate flood.

                                        1932.1

WINDOW 1[1]

Something sad and cold
    shimmers at the glass.
When I listlessly draw near
    and blur clouds of breath,
As if tamed it flutters frozen wings.
Though again and again I wipe and take a look,
The pitch black night—
    surging out, surging in—
        collides.
Drenched stars, agleam, are set like jewels.
To wipe the glass alone at night,
A lonely, spellbound meditation—
Ah, lovely lungs all torn,
You've flown away like a wild bird!

                           1930.1
                        (1929.12)

[1]This poem was written after the death of a child of the poet.

WINDOW 2

I peer out,
And in the pitch dark night,
A pine tree looms ever large
    before the bleak courtyard.
I return to my mat.
My throat is dry.
Approaching once more,
I peck at the pane with my lips.
Ah, stifled like a goldfish in a bowl!
A whistling night without moisture or stars;
A window that quakes like a little steamboat.
Violet crystal hailstones,
Draw out this naked body,
    pummel it, blister it!
My fever rises.
All the more tenderly, my cheeks
Nuzzle the pane and drink a cold kiss.
The faint smarting sound of a
    striking match—
Far-off flowers!
In the town rises a lovely fire.

1931.1

THE MOON

In an instant! Eyes wide awake,
    window brim full,
The moon surges like the rising tide.

I cast off my pillow and mind-benumbing sleep;
And, though no one calls, I'm called and go out.

To my lone gaze in the dead of night,
The yard, like a lake, brims to overflowing!

A white stone crouched to the side
Has a brow so lovely and smooth—

The green shade, once ardent and fair,
    and now dense with black ink,
Breathes tangled soughs
    as if sunk in weary slumber.

Cooing, cooing, the dove—
    why so restless?
Paulownia trees in bloom—
    unbearable fragrance!

1932.6

STARS 1

As I gaze lying down, a star,
So very far!

And yet near, as if
        linked by gold thread
To the corners of dimly drooping eyes.

Deep in the night, my sleep gently broken,
It presses against the pane for a peek!

Suddenly, as if welling up,
As if inviting a call,
        as if giving welcome,

Out of nowhere a lonely fire
Rises in my soul with remorse
        that surges like the wind.

I rise in white nightclothes
And fold my hands on my breast.

                                        1933.9

STARS 2

I open the window and lie down—
Since the window must be open
    for the sky to come in.

I put on spectacles I'd removed—
The night after a sun's eclipse,
    stars are all the more blue.

On a night feasting the stars,
I keep form with white dress and white mat.

Love with a wife in the world—
Compared with the stars, an untidy roost.

Turning on my side,
I sail, chartless, from star to star.

As stars rise in clusters,
One shines more lavish;

One faintly flickers,
As if newborn;

One, shimmering red,
Must radiate heat.

Even the stars are swept by winds—
Revolving, reviving candles!

Washed in cold water,
Spilling gold dust—
    the silver currents of the Milky Way!

Islands have ever run up beneath a mast;
And stars yearn for dusky harbor
        beneath our eyebrows.

The Great Bear
Revolves at a tilt!

In the tragedy of a magnificent sky,
We curb even the sound of breathing;

Be there cause or not in the other world,
We have a night when none can bare
        to close their eyes.

Without even a lullaby,
Sleep comes.

                                        1941.9

WINDOW

A day
Without a redwing
Wanes.

Frozen boughs hung with icicles
Are pierced by the sagging sky.

On the old pond—
        not even a sunken star—
Withered lotus stems
        moan in the wind.

In far-off fields,
No grass fires rise.

After the landscape,
Lavishly,
Has gone all away,

At my window
Again comes the dark,
Lovely like vapor.

1942.1

FROM "THE HEART'S DIARY"

One of Nine *Sijo*[1]

As the night wears on, this heart gets thin.
It will end up a thin, cold needle;
And I've no thread, no colored thread.

1926.6

LAKE 1

A face
Can take shelter
Deep in two hands,

But the longing heart,
Large as a lake—
Can only shut the eyes.

1930.5

FALLING STAR

I kept in mind

Where the star fell,

To go the next day.

I intended to go, intended to go,

And now I'm all grown up.

1930.10

[1]A *sijo* is a traditional Korean poetic form.

CAFE FRANCE

Stone lamps atilt
Beneath transplanted palms—
Off for Cafe France!

This chap, a *rubashka*;[1]
Another chap, a Bohemian cravat;
Leading the troupe, just a bag of bones.

Night rain fine as snake eyes,
Shafts of light panting on the pavement—
Off for Cafe France!

This guy's head, a skewed crab apple;
Another's heart, a worm-eaten rose;
One drenched chap darts like a swallow.

"Oh, Master Parrot! Good Evening!"

"Good Evening!"

Mademoiselle Tulip, tonight too,
Drowses beneath the silk curtain!

Not a viscount's son, not anything—
Hands so white, I'm sad!

No country, no home—
Against the marble table,
        my cheeks, sad!

O-oh, foreign puppy,
Lick my feet!
Lick my feet!

                                        1926.6

[1]*Rubashka*: a blouse-like garment worn by Russian men and
previously sometimes by painters.

RAYS OF THE EVENING SUN

Though I take a gulp
Of fiery liquor, ah, I'm hungry!

Though I crunch and munch
At the glass set shy there, I'll be hungry.

Your eyes are haughty black buttons;
Your lips, an indifferent bit of
    autumn watermelon.

Though I suck and suck, I'll be hungry.

The sunset's crimson rays at the
    tavern window
Ardently burn—ah, so hungry!

1930.5
(1926)

PEBBLES

Pebbles rolling, rolling . . . .
Are they pieces of my soul?

At one with the grief
        of an ailing Pierrot
And the grumbling, pent-up chatter
        of blue swallows
Bushed from first flight,
I sigh as I roam—
Pinched bruises still swollen red—
Down a strange foreign road
Flying with rain.

Pebbles rolling, rolling . . . .
Are they pieces of my soul?

                                        1932.7

CATHOLIC CHURCH

I walk listlessly up to a window and stand mute.
The pane of glass that cools my forehead is cold;
The end of the pencil I vapidly chew puckers my
        mouth.

                                        1940.1

TRAGEDY

Have you ever seen the fair face of tragedy?
That caller's visage is indeed lovely!
People get needlessly flustered by the exalted
    visit veiled in black.
So fragrant, in fact, are the traces of his passage,
That only long afterward does one know he has gone,
    leaving gifts of peace, sadness, and love.
He treads with caution, as if tracking a leopard,
So that sharp ears know only his knock.
Even tonight, ink gone dry and poem unwritten,
I'm prepared to meet him.
I've already given a daughter and son;
So if tonight he should forget his manners and come,
I'll gently decline at the gate.

                                      1935.3

The Christian Imagination

THE SEA OF GALILEE

My heart is
A little Sea of Galilee.

The constantly restless waves
Form not a beautiful scene.

Of old, the disciples
Woke the sleeping Lord.

By just waking the Lord,
Their faith became blessing.

The sail again unfurled;
The rudder regained course.

That today, too, in my
    little Sea of Galilee,
The Lord deliberately sleeps—

Only after the wind and sea get calm
Do my sighs understand!

1933.9

ANOTHER SKY

Though my eyes know not his features,
In him I naturally breathe sweet.

Born again in water and the Spirit—
Each day, a new sun!

Amid a noisy, motley generation,
I'll cherish the work he's done just for me.

A world as yet not had—
I would hardly expect it now.

The soul—fire and love!
        The body—sheer torture!
The seen sky, just a cover for my tomb.

Though the edge of his garment
        hasn't pierced my senses,
In the shade of his care
        I'll see my other sky.

1934.2

GRACE

Remorse, too—
A sacred grace.

The spring sun's rays,
      fine as silk threads,
Split ravine-hardened ice.

Tears brimming
From a needle-like smart

Quench bewitching hell-fires
Flickering beneath the ears.

For whom do ardent sighs
      pierce the heart?
In a stifled soul
      again settles love's dew.

Ah, to sink my bones
      in remorse!
Just to ache!

                                    1933.9

THE TREE

Face lifted straight
    toward the blue sky,
It's no shame that the feet point
    ever toward black earth.

Though grain falls headlong,
    the sprouts, ever upward!
In what form was it planted?
    A strange tree, my body!

A fitting position!
    Good above and below!
Adam's sad heritage
    accepted as it is.

In the scant years that mark my life,
    I number Israel's two-thousand years.
My being has been nothing but
    a chaffing flaw in the universe.

As a parched deer seeks a spring
    to dip its lips,
I drench my forehead in the sacred blood
    of Christ's nail-driven feet—

O-oh! I grasp in my arms the New Covenant sun.
                            1934.3

THE HOUR OF DEATH

The night of my final hour,
Let not a single cricket sing.

Let the priest who hears
    my sins for the last time
Sever my soul like a holy midwife.

Yellow candle from the Mass
    of Mary's Purification![1]

Along with sunflowers bowed above the wall,
Let it turn in yearning
    for another world's sun.

Halo worn by the good Lord Jesus,
Who comes as pay for a wayfarer's
    road to eternity,
Sow in my soul a seven-hued rainbow!

Agony of my life and last days,
Turn to fire in love's white-gold crucible!

Let me call on the sweet, sweet name
    of the Blessed Mother
Till my lips catch fire.

1933.9

[1]According to traditional Catholic practice, candles were blessed on the Feast of the Purification, February 2.

HALF OF HIM[1]

Him, how to name him?
Sweet fire in my soul,
Moon shining on a respectful brow,
A being more precious than my eyes,
The planet Venus rising from the sea
        with quivering wings,
High mountain plants dangling white blossoms
        in an indigo sky.
He stays not in my branches.
He is far from my land.
Always the distant one,
        sole in his own lovely freedom,
While I know not love and just hang my head.
From time to time, hands folded at my breast
As I tread anxiety's meandering twilight path,
I—, I sweetly cherish being the half of him
Left on this side of the sea.

                                        1931.10

[1]This poem does not employ specifically Christian imagery and
appeared earlier than poems that do so; yet the overall situation
suggests possible Christian overtones.

In The Mountains

THE SUMMIT

A rock cliff
Stamped in red cinnabar,
A dewlike flow of water,
A redwing plucking food
On a dangerous perch.
Shoots of wild grape slip past,
And a fragrant flower snake[1]
Curls up in a highland dream.
A majestic brow, huge, corpse-like—
Where seasonal birds first return,
Where the waxing moon disappears,
Where twin rainbow spans tred.
Seen from below, high as Orion.
I now stand at the peak.
Starlike white blossoms sway;
Like dandelions, the two spans stand trim;
The East Sea[2] at sunrise
Flutters at my cheeks
Like a distant flag toward the wind!

                                        1930.10

[1]Flower snake: the Korean expression for a colorful snake.
[2]The East Sea of Korea: the Sea of Japan.

PIRO PEAK 1[1]

The season hunkers down
In the huddled recesses
    of a birch forest.

This place, desolate site
    of a fleshless banquet—
Aromatic sustenance soaking the brow!

Above a five-thousand-foot layer
    of cirrus clouds
Flares a match!

The East Sea[2] stirs not—
    a print done in blue—
While beads of hail shift like bees.

Stripped even of shadows,
Ardor coolly freezes!
    Like a cricket.

                                        1933.6

[1]Piro Peak: the highest peak of Kŭmgang (Diamond) Mountain, in the northern part of Korea.
[2]East Sea: the Sea of Japan.

PIRO PEAK 2

The ivy
Turns color;

The chipmunk's tail,
A lush dark.

Autumn path
High in the mountains . . . .

Right above the brow,
The sun itself is fragrant.

Staff
Tap-tapping,

White fields
Laugh.[1]

Birch slip off
Their outward show;

And billowing clouds
Asleep by the flowers

Feel empty
In the breeze.

1938.8

[1]These two lines could also mean: "White fields / Cry."

WATERFALL

Even water bred in a mountain ravine
Got seized with fright at
    the sheer cliff drop-off.

Dozing by a bank of snow,
It took a turn beneath flowering trees

And in a hollow where crayfish crawl
Felt cramped beneath the tiny bit of sky.

Suddenly teetering,
No way but panic!

White claws scratching to shreds,
Devilishly cute—

Still, it chatters too much!
Sent plummeting, even water
    is scared at once to death.

On a day when
    deep in the mountains
Ferns are lulled all asleep,

Pine pollen
Streams yellow.

A pair of newlyweds
    out for the scenery
Blush like cherries.

Here we are! Jagged rocks,
    ever winding path—
Pretty as a picture.

My sun, too, round
Since Heine's time,

Tagging along all the day,
Just barely keeps up with
    clusters of heels.

The water of a falls
    tucked away in the mountains
Must needs descend creeping,
    creeping, in fear.

                          1936.7

OKRYU VALLEY[1]

The valley sky
Opens wide,

And waterfalls
Roar rumbling spring thunder.

Branched warp, ply on ply—
Like folded peony petals.

Peaks jutting precarious,
As if to shift and softly settle.

On and on, valley folding deep,
A jumbled, keen blue din of mist.

The sun, spreading wings,
As if smeared with pollen, soaring.

When swaths of violet sunbeams
Spread out aslant,

A hubbub of herbs
Drawing breath on lower slopes!

Broad day, when field birds fly not
And mystery holds full fair.

Water doesn't soak,
But roles over white stones;

And all along the way
      one's collar is tart
With soaking aromas.

Even crickets,
As if helplessly drunk,

Cease
Wriggling.

1937.11

KUSŎNG VALLEY[2]

Often, falling stars
Get buried in the dell.

Where hail piles up
With a din in the twilight

And flowers
Live in exile,

An old temple-site—
When winds are still

And mountain shadows
      form a loose weave,
Deer get up and cross the ridge.

1938.8

[1]Okryu Valley: Flowing Jade Valley.
[2]Kusŏng Valley: Nine Fortress Valley, an area of Kŭmgang (Diamond) Mountain in the north of Korea.

A SHORT PIECE OF MUSIC

In the dead of night
When water birds have
        folded their wings in sleep,

The azaleas among the rocks
        of Myŏngsu Pavilion—
A blaze of crimson!

Water coming, water going—
Ever sent right along, water on its way.

At heart a fickle fellow,
The wind gives a kiss and goes.

Though they blossom on stubs
Every year in season,

On a morning
When field birds fly in
        and shed tears of sorrow,

Petals withering,
        frivolously scattering,
Borne along the blue stream—
        how sad!

Too precious to lose,
Lovely spring night in its prime.

Light a candle; make it bright.
How not but be crimson!

                                                1938.6

¹Myŏngsu Pavilion: Clear Water Pavilion.

SPRING SNOW

The minute the door opens,
The mountain in the distance
    chills the brow!

On First Rain Day,[1]
The first morning of the month,

My brow bumps, bright and cool,
The mountain capped again with snow.

Ice cracking and wind slipping in anew,
My white clothes-tie, of itself, is fragrant.

An air of huddled survival,
So sad for its dreaminess!

Dropwort shoots sprouting green
And once-dormant fish lips awiggle,

In an unseasonable snow before blossom time,
I want to doff padded clothes
    and again be cold.

                                                    1939.4

[1]First Rain Day: February 19, one of twenty-four seasonal days
calculated by the sun. The second of these days after Lunar New
Year, this day marks the spring warming trend.

RAIN

The stones
Brim with shade.

Gusts of
Chilly spring winds.

Tail darting up,
Sure of the lead,

Rough-legged, quickstepping,
A mountain bird's gait.

Rapids form—
Gaunt white water—

Stretching fingers
To shreds.

Seeming to cease,
Sheets of rain break out anew!

Tramping loudly
Along leaf after ruddy leaf.

1941.1

BREAKFAST

With the sun
Fully bloomed,

Billowing clouds,
Shifting from dell to dell.

Bellflower buds
Get rinsed as they sway.

From quartz jags,
A sprinkling as of
        sprouting bamboo.

At the water's sound,
Teeth tingle.

Taking a place
Crouched toward the sun,

I become a heartsick bird
And peck grains of white rice.

                                    1941.1

HONEYSUCKLE TEA[1]

Honeysuckle tea drunk at all hours
Goes down the guts of the old proprietor.

An imposing birch fire
Blazes again scarlet.

As shade forms in nooks,
Radishes sprout green.

The earth's scent warm,
        its vapors coil
And in the sound of the wind-driven snow
        are still.

Deep in the mountains, without a calendar,
The long months of winter are white.

                                        1941.1

[1]The Chinese characters that make up the word "honeysuckle"
literally mean "braving the cold."

The Prose Poems

HOT SPRINGS

Wind now occupies the distant ravine we've put behind us since morning. As if caught, as it blows, in the bent branches of the tree out front, wind beats at the window! As the night wears on, the fire in the pot is a sorry sight; and the candle's eyelids are dim as from the cold. Bright through the night, my eyes keep watch where I lie. Your warm words brought sleep straight away and carried me off to a homely pillow. Now that you've gone, nothing for me but to opt anew for good sense and loneliness! Splitting the earth, gushing, gathering, ever hot from time immemorial, the water chatters alone in the dark, while a scattering of snow sails along the starless road.

1938.4

POOCH

The pooch that guarded your night the other night is sure a winsome fellow. The thick briar fence was closed tight; and behind the gate and sliding door, the candle light played in silent vigil. With snow piled in inches, the narrow path showed no trace of man. Did he bark that way because he was keen to something and couldn't settle down? Was he somehow uneasy lest there creep in the sound of the gurgling brook, boring through pebbles beneath the ice? lest there blithely step down the late night moon, brimming round from behind a huge peak? The pooch may well act up like that; but do I look like I'll touch so much as your things, let alone your person? The dog barks, then promptly curls in his showy beard, and, guarding the toes of the pretty shoes you've removed, falls asleep!

1938.4

CHANGSU MOUNTAIN[1] 1

It's said to be the din of downing trees; and it could well be the felling of a huge pine, girth greater than arms can grasp. The valley roars with what may well be the clang of resounding echoes. No chipmunks chasing, no mountain birds singing, deep mountain silence numbs the bone even more. Snow and the night are whiter than paper! And the moon—is its white intent as it awaits fullness a stroll through the valley in the dead of night? Now that the monk from the upper temple lost six out of six, laughed, and went up, is the moon gathering the scent left by the homespun old chap? Though anxiety reels in the windless silence, oh, I'll bear it. On Changsu Mountain, cold, heedless, without sorrow or dreams, through a deep winter's night . . . .

1939.3

CHANGSU MOUNTAIN 2

A mountain of stone without a quiver of grass, winding as a mass through twelve ravines! A cold sky covers each ravine; and, ice frozen firm, stepping stones seem safe. I set my feet in tracks trod by scrambling pheasants and tramping bears. The water chirps like crickets! In the flickering sunlight, snow settles on snow. White fringes draw breath, crushed beneath white fringes. Settling throughout the mountain, won't the profusion of fringes get hurt? I fling myself down upon a hazy cliff site once shadowed red with azaleas!

1939.3

[1]Changsu Mountain: Long Life Mountain.

PAENGNOK LAKE[1]

1

The closer you get to the top, the more worn away are the cornflowers. Climb one ridge, and the waists disappear; up another ridge, the necks are gone; and after that, just faces peep out, like a flowered print. Where the wind's cold vies with the tip of Hamgyŏng Province,[2] cornflowers have no height at all. Yet they abound for a while in August like scattered stars. When mountain shadows darken, stars light up as well in the cornflower fields, moving with their constellations. I'm here, exhausted.

2

I moisten my throat with the pretty pill-like fruit of the crowberry and get up, refreshed.

3

White birch live beside white birch till they're skeletons. Like birch, my whiteness when dead will not be unscarred.

4

On a mountain spur too desolate even for ghosts, lone flowering beggar-ticks blanch with fear even in broad day.

5

At almost 6,000 feet, horses and cattle live without a thought of humans. Horses with horses, cows with cows, colts after mother cows, calves after mother horses—all follow one another, promptly to part.

6

The cow had an awfully hard time giving birth to its first calf. In a moment of bewilderment, she turned down a mountain path for a hundred *ri*[3] and ran off for Sŏgwip'o.[4] Still not dry and its mother gone, the calf cried "ma-a, ma-a." Horses, mountaineers—it clung to them at random. I cried to think that our brood, too, might be left to a mother whose coat has a different hue.

7

The scent of wind orchids, the sound of orioles calling back and forth, whistling Cheju warblers, water tumbling off rocks, the swish of eddying winds as the sea crumples in the distance . . . . I go astray among ash, camellia, and oak, only to find myself once again on a winding path packed with white stones and crawling with arrowroot vines. A dappled horse, all at once right before me, doesn't budge!

8

Fern, *tŏdŏk*[5] sprouts, bellflowers, asters, rain-hat shoots, bamboo grass, mushrooms, high mountain plants that dangle starlike bells—etching them in my heart, drunk with them, I sleep. The procession that forms above the mountain range in yearning for the plain water of Paengnok Lake is more stately than the clouds. Caught in a mat of rain, dried out in a rainbow,[6] and flower juice worked into the rump, my flesh swells.

9

In the blue water of Paengnok Lake, where not even crayfish crawl, the sky revolves. Past my legs nearly crippled with fatigue, a cow makes a detour and goes its way. With the mere hint of thread-like clouds chased this way, Paengnok Lake blurs. Folded towards my face the whole day long, Paengnok Lake is desolate. Waking and drowsing, I've forgot even to pray.

1939.4

¹Paengnok Lake: White Deer Lake, a crater lake at the top of Halla Mountain on Cheju Island, the island province at the southern tip of Korea.

²Hamgyŏng Province: the province at the furthermost tip of the north of Korea.

³*Ri*: a Korean measure of distance, about four-tenths of a kilometer.

⁴Sŏgwip'o: a harbor city on Cheju Island.

⁵*Tŏdŏk*: a plant with a bell-like flower and an edible root.

⁶The Korean can also mean: "rolled up in a rainbow."

AZALEAS

In one valley, rain; in another, wind. In one valley, I pick a trail through the shade; in another, through the sun. A valley hung with a rainbow atilt in the spreading sun, a valley whirling and buzzing with swarms of wild bees formed into gourds, a valley where I cautiously creep round the scent of a napping tiger hidden in the red and yellow tangles of a scrub-tree forest and come out alive. I climb the highest peak and pick up a stone cleaner than the stars. Above white birch branches the sky so blue . . . . The hurl awhirr . . . . All over the mountain, red leaves rustle. Entering the unlit side room of a lower temple, I heat a wood pillow and idly sear blisters on my soles. Then I curse that devil of a tiger and at once lie down. Heedless of the sound of water by my pillow, I slip out into a valley, where I encounter a sudden, unseasonable flood of azaleas. All crimson, I halt.

1941.1

BUTTERFLY

A job done unbidden wants haste. I renew the stove fire with fresh ash wood. Puff, puff—I polish the lamp globe, attach it, flip up the sputtering wick; and the flame buds anew. When I tear off a page early and hang up the calendar, tomorrow's date is already red. Autumn sky in the offing, above the chain of peaks I'll be trekking across on a path twisting out like a chipmunk's back-seam. Night in a mountain cabin stripped of fallen leaves, sounding a second-hand's strange ticktock. As clouds haunt the night panes, the drip-drop sound of water.

Hugging close, a butterfly big as the palm of a hand peeps in. Pitiful! Making a fist, it bangs at the unopened window; and the four walls, with no breath to fly, quiver all the more with the wings. This freehand sketch awkwardly stuck as it breathes a bit of rain-washed fantasy swirling at 5,000 feet—how it envies the strange season encased in the bright blazing flame. Wings all torn, if it should open black eyes like a monkey[1]—how scary!

Clouds shatter crag-like again against the glass, and stars sweep below. Above what village down the mountain do they twinkle? Pearl-white peak of lolling groves of birch, dusky milk-white night.

                                                                1941.1

[1]Monkey: There is a pun here with the word for butterfly.

SWALLOWTAIL BUTTERFLY

He shouldered his art gear, went on and on into the massed mountains, and soon his footprints got faint. The autumn colors fade; every peak scowls; snow flies; and the inner and outer doors of the ridge-pass shop are closed—unopened the whole winter long. Past the turn of the year and deep into spring, the snow reaches the eaves. Above a large canvas, the cotton-like clusters of last year's white clouds glide anew; the sound of waterfalls plays louder and louder; blue skies return. But, shoes and slippers still set side by side,[1] love starts to reek raw. The odor spread at the window of each house that night with the evening paper. Though the people of Kosŏng[2] in Hoeyang County know the plain, fair face of the widow from Hakkatta,[3] the painter turned shopkeeper hasn't even a name. Pine pollen is yellow—cuckoo, cuckoo—flowering ferns bend, and swallowtail butterflies pair off and flutter across the green mountains.

1941.1

[1]According to Korean custom, shoes are left outside the house at the porch steps.

[2]Kosŏng: a town on the east coast of Korea.

[3]Hakkatta: the business district of Fukuoka, Japan.

BOOTLEG DIGGING

Even after a hundred days' prayer, the mountains yielded no ginseng. In a flash of the birch bonfire, between bellflowers, *tŏdŏk*,[1] and aster buds, there swayed to and fro a wild ginseng[2] shoot. Smoking throw-away tobacco leaves, the old ginseng hunter cushioned his head on a stone. He dreamt that night that the ginseng plant, petite like a good second wife,[3] girded up fuchsia skirts and wrapped around his cuddly, puffed-out breast. He awakes. Seeming to sink, the fire on the sands revives. Between the narrowed eye of the constable and the bright blaze in the distance, the bead of the rifle drew straight. In the black starless night, the gunfire was beautiful like fuchsia dye. A chipmunk curled up in a ball and scurried away.

1941.1

[1] *Tŏdŏk*: a plant with a bell-like flower and an edible root.

[2] Wild ginseng is more highly prized than the cultivated variety. Traditionally only men could hunt for it, and only after a hundred days of prayer. During the years of Japanese occupation of Korea, hunting it in the mountains was outlawed. Ginseng is said to be an aphrodisiac.

[3] Second wife: It was formerly acceptable for a man of the upper class to maintain in his household a "second wife," either as a mistress or to provide for a male heir.

FORMAL ATTIRE

There was a middle-aged gentleman who attired himself formally in morning coat, went out into the Taemanmul Mountains,[1] and leapt from Kumanmul Peak.[2] On the way down, his outer jacket caught on a pine branch; and stripped as he was in just his shirt, he lay flat on his stomach lest his necktie suffer harm. Settling, settling through the dead of winter, the snow's white palm gave cover. "Since I'll not be breathing," thought the middle-aged man, "it won't be cold"; and in a proper corpse-like rite, he lay prostrate the whole winter long. In folds like the formal attire, the snow's whiteness vanished with the fullness of spring.

1941.1

[1]Taemanmul Mountains: Myriad Nature Mountains, an area in the Kŭmgang (Diamond) Mountains in the northern part of Korea. The area is noted for its fantastical rock formations.
[2]Kumanmul Peak: Old Myriad Nature Peak.

A COVERED CARRIAGE

At the watch-shop corner that I'm just going round, rascals called larks that hang from the eaves by day, old as they are to the city's ways, chatter away in husky voices toward where people stream down.

That appearance of drowsy exhaustion, eyes drooping—a speck, shall I say, of piteous sleep—rises in my heart, a heart with nowhere to cling, that wants to caress and be caressed. My pitiful shadow, like black funeral garb, streams aimlessly down. Under a drenched, ribbonless poet's chapeau, the evening scene, like a torrent of goldfish, streams on down. With a tread as of foreign scouts, ginkgo saplings lined up along the road stream silently, silently down.

> Blurring sad silver spectacles,
> The night rain paints, sidelong, a rainbow.

My little soul flutters, as if surprised by the sound of an occasional late streetcar that creaks its way round the bend. I want to go. I want to seek warmth by an open stove. I want to shell Nanjing beans as I read my beloved Koran. But do I have such a place to return to?

At the tower that shoots briskly up from the red-brick house at the crossroads, an arrogant twelve o'clock points solemn fingers up at the lightning rod. My neck, too, now seems about to plummet! What fun it would be to look down from on high and see myself strolling in the shape of a pine needle. Shall I relax and take a smooth piss? The helmeted night-watch is sure to come and—just like the movies—chase me away!

The red wall at the crossroads is soaked, the cheeks of the woebegone city wet. My heart makes listless scribblings of love. What wells up alone with tears is the eye of a red lamp shining on the wretched lot of Sonia. Were our nights in days gone by just as sad, just as lonely? Well, shall I just fold my hands on my breast here and await you?

All slush, the road glistens with something like snake eyes. Drowsiness sets in as I walk, perhaps because of my oversized shoes. They threaten to stick fast in the mud. I've a reckless longing, a longing for your curved shoulders. My head on your shoulders, there always comes the sound of a warm distant sea-wail . . . . . .

. . . . Ah, long though I wait, unable to come . . . .

One unable to come though I wait. So my drowsy heart calls a covered carriage, a carriage that, called, comes like a whistle. I await a covered carriage spread with the down of lovebirds and bearing silver sorrow, a carriage just as lovely as you—slosh, slosh—a covered carriage!

1927.6
(1925.11)

MELANCHOLY IDOL

Are you at peace this night?
Though I ask myself, all alone, how you fare, could I
possibly address you in plain rude words?

Does there not exist, in some words or other, a language
that elevates you a bit higher, that better becomes you?

You! —who'll be slumbering more lovely than a dove
with eyes closed, than buds composed in sleep for the idle
hours of a flower's shifting shadow.

Shall I take your eyes for illustration?
A pair of lakes, to the depths clear and blue.
Does night exist to nest steeped in these lakes?
Could I dare act as the evening star and submerge in
your lakes?

The neatly composed margins of your lips—oh, lest
decorum crumble, I'll collect myself and elucidate.

The grounds are various; but in the end there's reason
augustly to revere you and fear you like a leopard.

If there hopes to remain a sacred peak still clear of
others' tracks, still to be climbed, it's your nose, all the whiter
in snow. To your misfortune, though the season be lush, you
thus always scent only the fragrance of alpine flora.

Reverently, cautiously, I shall raise my eyes to your fore-
head, pass again by your cheeks, and reach ears just barely
concealed in your ebony black hair.

Seashells, seen before in Greece at the Ionian Sea—though poised ever to listen, what they heard remained unknown.

A sea tranquil as oil, the bluest of skies, sands so white that resting gulls went unseen. Seashells, in silence, opening leisurely listening ears at a time when I found nothing there to hear—from that hour on, I've known what it is to be an utterly forlorn wayfarer.

This world, in the end, no more than an empty shell—though skies serve as cover and seas circle round, it's all no more than the shell of another world.

The sea shells' silent listening was, indeed, the affair of another world. And how could I not but turn mournfully away?
The sound of the wind as well made no sense; it wandered about with just barely a stammer.

Straying about your ears, I'm no more than a wayfarer about to disappear, forlorn.
For your ears, again tonight, just lie open with attentive grace!
Even in this noisy world, circling round your ears I see only the Ionian Sea, silent as a corpse.

I shall now make bold to enter once more your most inner recesses.

As the sea keeps hoarded in its depths an endless variety of mystic coral, so are you stocked within with things precious and rare.
The first wonder is how you preserve such a depth of goodness.

Your heart—what a rarity!

No doubt because she emerged unadorned with this heart, even the Muse, peerless masterpiece born of the hands of the master-craftsman Greece, ended up passing dreary days in art museums. How do you come by such a possession?

A crucible more precious than white gold, bearing forever life's sacred flame; a sanctuary enshrining the timeless love-heritage of heaven and earth.

The constantly gorgeous crimson of its color gives proof.

But since your heart most readily sensed shame on the rare occasions when you opened a window to the world, it has hidden within for good.

And how lovely and fresh are your lungs; how profound and enchanting, your liver and gall!

This isn't the place, though, for prolonged discussion of their color.

There are areas, besides, that could be elucidated in terms of streams flowing in sequestered vales and mysterious rivers; but I must survey these broadly and pass on.

And there's a pair to be likened to small hills, supple and curved like the sun rising, the moon floating, the jade rabbit[1] drowsing, bounding.

With this and that illustration, I'll lose the way and wander like a wayfaring stranger in a labyrinth.

But already gathered together, curled up, arranged, and massed with perfect design and equipoise, are you not folding your ivory hands and nobly crossing your legs?

You thus bring wisdom, prayer, and breath into perfect accord.

When I expound on the absolute beauty of your person, however, I cannot but reflect as well on your site and surroundings.

Though repetition is bothersome, ultimately this world, like an empty shell, amounts to nothing. How have you entrusted just here in its midst your castle of solitude?

How have you come to take limpid sorrow as your cushion of repose?

Since for me it's all so sad, I circle your solitary castle with the cold wan moon in the dead of night like a glum shaggy dog that can't even bark. I circle on guard, and I sigh.

I shake with the premonition that the morning will soon come when out of love, solitude, and devotion, you'll rid yourself of your four limbs of beauty, virtue, and splendor,

O-oh, of the mass of your radiant elegance, and be plucked away.

Will your ears still open that morning with a listening grace like the white shells by the Ionian Sea?

Presenting a white lily as a final adornment, I, too, shall depart the Ionian shores.

1938.3

[1]Jade rabbit: According to Korean legend, a jade rabbit lives on the moon.

The Last Poems

YOU RETURN![1]

The people and nation
Sold off to barbarians,
A demon arrogantly ensconced
In the National Shrine—
Thirty-six years,
Darker than a corpse!

You return!
Fruit of spilt blood,
　　　radiantly return!

You mountains stripped of finery,
That stand turned away alone,
Turn now aright!
Waters off course,
Flow in old beds with a new sound!
It's not yesterday's sky—
Let a new sun ascend.

You return!
Fruit of spilt blood,
　　　radiantly return!

Furrows razed,
Grain looted,
Nothing to offer.
No welcoming silks!
Just uniforms
Dusty from combat.

You return!
Fruit of spilt blood,
   radiantly return!

Kinfolk scattered
By savage horse hoofs.
Venerable old fathers,
   brothers, little sisters—
Bleached bones tumbling
   strange and nameless about the earth.

At every still suddenly waiting village—
How should you tread flowers?
Make a path in tears through thorns!

You return!
Fruit of spilt blood,
   radiantly return!

                       1946.1

[1]This poem commemorates Korean independence from Japanese rule at the end of World War II.

UNTITLED

Though not to Rome,
The road has led by a straight way
That couldn't, just couldn't be otherwise!
What, then, of poetry
That rough, coarse, and uncomely though it be,
Knows no falsehood, no rash assault?

1949.1

CIRCUS TROOP

A place of refuge—
Though over snow
The wind not cold

A clarinet sounds
A drum beats
The tent flaps and pops
Flags fly—
A strangely sad, gala evening

A horse makes a run
And pierces a flaming hoop
On its back
A girl does a flip

A seal
Toots a horn

Not trapeze artistry
But dazzling somersaults
        in black space!

I spy a girl's legs
Fresh like cabbages

Arms folded, a weight lifter
Rides a unicycle

In the dressing room
        a baby cries
In and out goes Jerry[1]
        in a green-ribboned bob

A monkey
Lights a cigarette

In my winter hat and coat
A forlorn child of forty years ago

I stand by my daughter of sixteen
Who's more of an adult
Than ten-year-old me

On the soles of a girl's feet
        twirls a fifty-foot pole
At the top of the pole
        a boy does a headstand
On his feet twirls a plate
The pole wavers
The plate precariously bounces

The clarinet sounds
The drum beats

The leather-coated ring-master
—Hurrah! hurrah!—
        leads the cheer

In my winter hat and coat
My utterly perilous forty-ninth year
Spins with the plate and I clap.

                                                                    1950.2

[1]Jerry: In years past, it was not uncommon in Korea to call a young tumbler, boy or girl, "Jerry."

Five Verses in Four-four Measure

AN OLD TIGER

An old tiger
Like me
Sits here
Before you
Just like your father
Though I were
Your father
Wouldn't I sit here
Before you
Just like a tiger?

YOUR FIGURE

If indeed
I were you
On a long
Winter's night
I'd sleep
Not a wink
Figure
So lovely
You'd treasure
Yourself so
How sleep?

FLOWER POT

The late winter cold
On the veranda
Halts "Ahem!"[1]
Right at your door

You clump
About
Heavy
As a pot

MOUNTAIN MOON

It's you
Mountain-moonlike
I can't
Enwomb you
It's me
Rabbitlike[2]
Frozen
I fall sleep

BUTTERFLY

Since
Like a butterfly
Soon I'll die
Just like a butterfly
Here I fly
Perched on the
Edge of your
Black silk dress
The window gets light
And away I fly

1950.6

[1]Traditionally, one does not knock to indicate one's presence, but lightly coughs.

[2]According to Korean legend, a rabbit lives on the moon.

Index of Titles and First Lines

Titles appear in italics, first lines in Roman type.